What's So Great About...?

JACQUES CARTIER

Marylou Morano Kjelle

P.O. Box 196
Hockessin, Delaware 19707
Visit us on the web: www.mitchelllane.com
Comments? email us: mitchelllane@mitchelllane.com

Printing   1   2   3   4   5   6   7   8   9

A Robbie Reader/What's So Great About . . . ?

Annie Oakley	Daniel Boone	Davy Crockett
Ferdinand Magellan	Francis Scott Key	Henry Hudson
Jacques Cartier	Johnny Appleseed	Robert Fulton
Sam Houston		

Library of Congress Cataloging-in-Publication Data
Kjelle, Marylou Morano.
    Jacques Cartier / by Marylou Morano Kjelle.
        p. cm. — (A Robbie Reader. What's so great about . . . ?)
    Includes bibliographical references and index.
    ISBN 1-58415-481-0 (library bound : alk. paper)
    1. Cartier, Jacques, 1491–1557—Juvenile literature. 2. Explorers—America—Biography—Juvenile literature. 3. Explorers—France—Biography—Juvenile literature. 4. Canada—Discovery and exploration—French—Juvenile literature. 5. Canada—History—To 1763 (New France)—Juvenile literature. 6. Northwest Passage—Discovery and exploration—French—Juvenile literature. I. Title. II. Series.
    E133.C3K57 2006
    971.01'13092—dc22
                                                                                    2005036701

ISBN-10: 1-58415-481-0   ISBN-13: 9781584154815

ABOUT THE AUTHOR: Marylou Morano Kjelle is a freelance writer and photo-journalist who lives and works in central New Jersey. She is a regular contributor to several local newspaper and online publications. She has written over 20 nonfiction books for young readers, including *Hilary Duff, Tony Hawk,* and *Francis Scott Key* for Mitchell Lane Publishers. Marylou has a master's of science degree from Rutgers University. She teaches English and writing at Rutgers and several other colleges in New Jersey.

PHOTO CREDITS: Cover—Stock Montage/Getty Images; pp. 1, 3, 8, 11, 13, 24, 26—Library of Congress; p. 4—Time Life Pictures/Mansell/Getty Images; pp. 6, 14, 17, 20, 22—North Wind Picture Archives; pp. 12, 18—Sharon Beck; p. 19—National Archives.

PUBLISHER'S NOTE: The following story has been thoroughly researched and to the best of our knowledge represents a true story. While every possible effort has been made to ensure accuracy, the publisher will not assume liability for damages caused by inaccuracies in the data, and makes no warranty on the accuracy of the information contained herein.

                                                                                    PLB

A Robbie Reader

TABLE OF CONTENTS

Words in **bold** type can be found in the glossary.

Like many explorers before him, Jacques Cartier set out looking for the Northwest Passage from Europe to China. Cartier first set sail in 1534, but almost 400 years passed before the Norwegian explorer Roald Amundsen actually crossed the Northwest Passage. Amundsen's voyage lasted from 1903 to 1906.

The Unknown Sea

In 1535, French explorer Jacques Cartier (ZJAHK KAR-tee-ay) was on a mission. He wanted to find the Northwest Passage. This route was a way to travel from Europe to China and other countries in eastern Asia by sailing west across the Atlantic Ocean. Many people, especially **European** traders, believed this shortcut existed. If Cartier could find it, then the traders would no longer have to sail around the tip of Africa to trade for spices in Asia.

Cartier had made his first voyage to the Americas a year earlier. At that time he had noticed a large body of water west of the Gaspé Peninsula. This body of water lies in what we now call Canada. Cartier believed this

Cartier leaves for one of his voyages to the New World on his flagship *Grande Hermine.* In 1534, Cartier set sail from St. Malo on the first of his three voyages to the Americas. The wooden ship weighed 60 tons and was 80 feet long. It held a crew of thirty men.

waterway, which he thought of as an "unknown sea," was the Northwest Passage he had been looking for. On his first trip, there had been no time to explore it. Cold weather had been on its way. Cartier and his crew did not have enough food and other **provisions** to survive the winter in Canada.

Now, a year later, Cartier was once again in the New World. With him were two young Wendat boys. The explorer had brought the boys back to France with him the year before. Now he was returning them to their tribe.

As Cartier steered his flagship, the *Grande Hermine,* onto the "unknown sea," the boys realized where they were. They told Cartier they were not sailing on a sea. They were sailing on a river they called the Hochelaga. It was a river so long that no Wendat had ever been to where it started.

Cartier was the first European to sail the mighty river, which later became known as the St. Lawrence. His discovery led the way for other French explorers to settle Canada and build the first French colonies in the Americas.

Christopher Columbus reaches the shores of San Salvador. Columbus was an Italian explorer who sailed for King Ferdinand and Queen Isabella of Spain. When Columbus landed on what is now known as San Salvador on October 12, 1492, he thought he had landed in India. Columbus called the new land the Indies. He called the people who lived there Indians.

Wondering About the World

Jacques Cartier was born in 1491 in St. Malo, a fishing port in northwestern France. At the time he was born, people were starting to become curious about the world. They wondered whether it was round or flat. They were eager to see what lands and riches lay beyond Europe and the Atlantic Ocean. One year after Jacques was born, Christopher Columbus became the first European to set foot in the Americas.

Jacques's father was a fisherman. At first young Jacques wanted to be a fisherman, too. As a boy, his fishing trips with his father may have taken him as far west as Newfoundland, an island discovered by John Cabot in 1497.

Jacques wanted to see more of the world. He wanted to explore new lands. When he was a young man, he went to Dieppe, another port in France. There he studied to be a **navigator**. One of his first voyages was sailing to Brazil on a Portuguese ship.

When Jacques Cartier was almost thirty years old, he married Catherine des Granches. She came from a family of shipbuilders. There is no record showing whether they had children.

Early explorers like Columbus and Cabot wanted to solve a puzzle. They were trying to find a new route from Europe to Cathay. Cathay was the name Italian explorer Marco Polo had given to China. The new route was called the Northwest Passage because explorers believed Cathay lay to the north and west of Europe, and on the other side of the Americas.

Explorers from Spain, Italy, Portugal, and England had all tried to find the Northwest

John Cabot discovers Newfoundland. Cabot was an Italian who explored "newfound lands" for England's King Henry VII. In 1497, Cabot landed on the island of Newfoundland. He was the first explorer to claim land in the Americas for England.

Passage, and they had all failed. However, some explorers, including the Spanish conqueror Vasco Núñez de Balboa, had found gold and other riches in the Americas. King

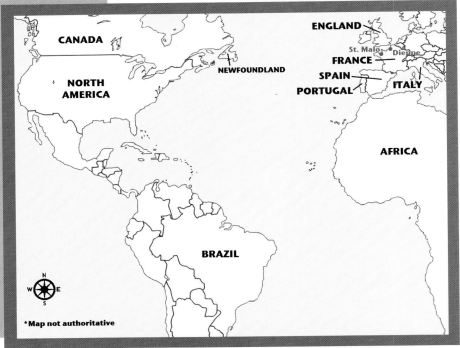

*Map not authoritative

Jacques Cartier spent his life around the sea. He was born in St. Malo, France, an important fishing town. He studied navigation at Dieppe, a major center for those who planned a life at sea. One of Cartier's first voyages was sailing to Brazil on a Portuguese ship.

Francis I of France wanted his country to share in the land and riches of the Americas, too.

The king needed a special navigator to explore the Americas for France. He chose Jacques Cartier. In 1534, he gave Cartier a **commission**. He sent him off to explore the Americas in the name of France.

In 1534, King Francis I commissioned Jacques Cartier to explore the Americas for France. Cartier's discovery of the Americas while Francis I was king (1515–1574) was one of France's finest accomplishments.

Cartier was forty-three years old. The most exciting adventure of his life so far was about to begin.

Jacques Cartier raises a 30-foot cross on the shore of Canada, claiming the land for France. The raising of the cross angered the natives, who saw it as a sign that their land would be taken away from them.

Claiming Land for France

Cartier and his crew of sixty men set sail for the Americas in April of 1534. They sailed on two small wooden ships. They brought along enough food to last about five months. The weather was good for sailing, and within twenty days, Cartier and his crew could see Cape Bonavista, a piece of land jutting out from the coast of Newfoundland.

Cartier explored land we now know as Canada. In these new places he saw many unusual sights. One such place was a small island off the coast of Newfoundland. Now it is called Funk Island, but in Cartier's time, it was known as the Isle of Birds. Thousands of birds lived there. "Unless a man did see this, he would think it an incredible thing," Cartier wrote.

Cartier continued sailing and eventually reached the area of Quebec known as the Gaspé Peninsula. There he met some Wendat (sometimes called Wyandot) people, a Native American tribe. Cartier studied these native peoples. "They have no other lodgings but their canoes which they turn up and sleep under on the ground. They eat their meat nearly raw . . . and also their fish," he wrote.

The Wendat told Cartier they lived in *kanata,* which was their word for "village." Cartier thought they were referring to the whole land. He called the region Canada.

At Cape Gaspé, Cartier claimed the Canadian lands he had discovered for King Francis I. He raised a thirty-foot cross on the shore. Attached to the cross was the French **emblem**. Carved into the cross's wooden bar were the words: *Long Live the King of France.*

Donnacona greets Cartier in friendship. The Native Americans living in Canada were at first happy to see Jacques Cartier and his crew sail to their shores. Cartier traded small trinkets from Europe for the furs of the animals the Native Americans had trapped. This is believed to be the beginning of fur trading between European explorers and America's native peoples.

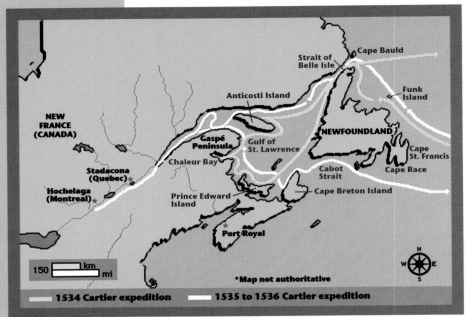

The first two of three voyages Jacques Cartier made to the Americas from France were in 1534 and 1535. He explored lands that are now present-day Newfoundland, Prince Edward Island, Quebec, Montreal, and Funk Island. In spite of all of these discoveries, Cartier is best known for his exploration of the Hochelaga, or St. Lawrence River.

The cross made the Wendat angry. They saw that Cartier was claiming their land. Cartier was able to reassure Donnacona, the chief of the Wendat village called Stadacona (today known as Quebec). He even asked Donnacona if he could take his two sons, Taignoagny and

Cartier holds a meeting with the Wendat people. When he arrived at the Gaspé Peninsula, he was greeted by members of the tribe. Although the Wendat were related to the Iroquois, they were often at war. The Iroquois eventually drove the Wendat into land that is today Ohio.

Domagaya, back to France with him. He wanted to teach them French so that they could act as **interpreters**. Donnacona gave his permission, and Cartier promised to bring the two boys back to Canada on his next voyage. The next day, Cartier and his crew set sail for France.

Cartier stands at the summit of Montreal. He sailed the St. Lawrence River to the foot of this mountain, which he called Mont Royal. It is in today's Montreal.

Return to the Americas

In May of 1535, Cartier again set sail for the Americas. This time, his fleet contained three ships and about one hundred sailors. They carried enough food and supplies to last fifteen months. Also on the journey were Taignoagny and Domagaya. As he promised, Cartier was returning them to Stadacona.

On August 10, 1535, the feast of St. Lawrence, Cartier and his ships were stopped at a bay near the island of Anticosti. A storm was keeping them from sailing on to the "unknown sea" that Cartier was sure would lead to China. Since it was the feast of St. Lawrence, Cartier named the bay the St. Lawrence Bay.

As soon as the storm stopped, Cartier's three boats sailed on to the sea. It was here

On his second voyage to the Americas, Cartier sailed the St. Lawrence River westward. Donnacona tried to stop Cartier from sailing. Three medicine men from his tribe dressed up as devils. They tried to scare Cartier, but he sailed the river anyway.

that Taignoagny and Domagaya told Cartier that the unknown sea was really a river. Cartier named it the River of Canada. Many years later it was given the name the St. Lawrence River, after the bay into which it emptied.

Cartier had his men set up a fort for the winter, near what is now Quebec City. Then he sailed westward to see how far the river ran. Cartier was amazed at the beauty of the land. "The whole country on both sides of this river . . . is a fine land," he wrote.

Cartier followed the river to the foot of a mountain, which he named Mont Royal. The name would later become Montreal. He could not follow the river to its starting point. At Montreal, the river became a series of rapids through which no ship could sail.

He was eager to return to France to tell the king all that he had seen in Canada on his second voyage. In May of 1536, he set sail for home. With him were Donnacona and nine other Wendat. Cartier had tricked some of these people into returning with him. Even so, he was reportedly kind to the captives he brought back with him to France.

Donnacona would never see his homeland again. He died in France in 1539.

Samuel de Champlain also tried to find the Northwest Passage, but, like Jacques Cartier, he was unsuccessful. In 1608 he settled Quebec. He also found one of the Great Lakes. It is named Lake Champlain after him.

Last Years

Cartier made his last voyage to the Americas in May 1541. He left France with five ships and enough provisions for two years. On board the ships were one thousand people who were planning to start French colonies in Canada.

The boats landed near what is now Quebec City, and a settlement was built. The winter of 1541 was a harsh one for the French pioneers, and the Wendat were no longer friendly to the French. The Wendat were angry at Cartier because their leader, Donnacona, had died in France and did not return to them. From time to time they attacked Cartier's new settlement, which was called Charlesbourg-Royal. About thirty-five settlers in all died in the

The Wendat help Champlain explore the Canadian wilderness.
Samuel de Champlain was friends with the Wendat. He helped them
fight the Iroquois.

raids. In the spring of 1542, Cartier set sail for France and did not return to the Americas again.

Jacques Cartier lived the rest of his life in or near St. Malo. He wrote a book about his travels. He was happy to tell his stories about the discovery of Canada to all who wanted to hear. He died on September 1, 1557. He was sixty-six years old.

After Cartier's last voyage to the Americas, France did not send explorers to Canada for many years. Then, in the early 1600s, France began to take an interest in "New France" once again. Explorer Samuel de Champlain traveled up the St. Lawrence River in 1608 and founded the city of Quebec. People began settling in Canada again.

Cartier started out looking for the Northwest Passage, and he ended up finding a new country. Although he did not discover the Northwest Passage, his voyages to the Americas prepared the way for the French to permanently settle in Canada. The **influence** of those early French settlers is felt even today.

CHRONOLOGY

1491   Jacques Cartier is born in St. Malo, France, on December 31.

1519   Cartier marries Catherine des Granches.

1534   Cartier makes his first voyage to the Americas. He erects a cross in the name of the King of France at Cape Gaspé, then returns to France.

1535   Cartier returns to the Americas and explores the St. Lawrence River.

1536   Cartier returns to France, bringing captives from the Wendat village of Stadacona.

1541   Cartier leaves for his third expedition into the Americas.

1542   Cartier returns to France. He does not go back to the Americas.

1557   Cartier dies on September 1 in St. Malo.

TIMELINE IN HISTORY

1271   Marco Polo is one of the first Europeans to visit China.

1487   Bartolomeu Dias discovers the southern tip of Africa.

1492   Christopher Columbus lands on San Salvador in the Bahamas.

1497   John Cabot discovers Newfoundland.

1502	Amerigo Vespucci discovers Brazil for Portugal while searching for the Northwest Passage.
1513	Vasco Núñez de Balboa claims the Pacific Ocean for Spain.
	Juan Ponce de Leon is the first European to set foot in Florida.
1519	Ferdinand Magellan sets off for a trip around the world.
1534	Jacques Cartier begins the first of three voyages to explore Canada.
1577– 1580	Sir Francis Drake sails around the world.
1609	Henry Hudson discovers the Hudson River while searching for the Northwest Passage.

FIND OUT MORE

Books

Blashfield, Jean F. *Cartier.* Minneapolis: Compass Point Books, 2002.

Harmon, Daniel. *Jacques Cartier and the Exploration of Canada.* Broomall, Pennsylvania: Chelsea House, 2000.

Humble, Richard. *Voyages of Jacques Cartier.* New York: Franklin Watts, 1993.

Works Consulted

Averill, Esther. *Cartier Sails the St. Lawrence.* New York: Harper & Row, 1956.

Cartier, Jacques. *Navigations to Newe Fraunce.* John Florio, trans. Ann Arbor: University Microfilms, Inc., 1966.

Cook, Ramsay. *The Voyages of Jacques Cartier.* Toronto: The University of Toronto Press, 1993.

Hoffman, Bernard G. *Cabot to Cartier.* Toronto: The University of Toronto Press, 1961.

On the Internet

Dictionary of Canadian Biography Online: "Jacques Cartier"
http://www.biographi.ca/EN/ShowBio.asp?BioId=34229

Passageways: *True Tales of Explorers for Young Adventurers,* "Jacques Cartier: New Land for the French King"
http://www.collectionscanada.ca/explorers/kids/h3-1321-e.html

PBS: *Empire of the Bay,* "Jacques Cartier"
http://www.pbs.org/empireofthebay/profiles/cartier.html

GLOSSARY

commission (kuh-MIH-shun)—an official document that gives someone the rank of an officer in the military.

emblem (EM-blum)—a picture with a unique design that indicates a specific group or organization.

European (yur-uh-PEE-un)—a person from Europe, a large area of the earth that includes the countries of England, Spain, Portugal, France, and others.

influence (IN-floo-uns)—the power to affect a person or event, usually as a result of wealth or position.

interpreter (in-TUR-preh-tur)—someone who helps translate conversations between people who speak different languages.

navigator (NAA-vih-gay-tur)—one who has knowledge of the sea and sailing and directs the course of a ship.

provisions (pruh-VIH-zhuns)—a stock of supplies needed to survive, such as food and water.

INDEX